ARE YOU RUGGED OR UNRUGGED?

A Graphic Guide to Ruggedtivity

RUGGED DUDE

BY THE ONLY MAN WITH THE NAME **Rugged Dude** ON HIS PASSPORT

ILLUSTRATIONS BY MURRAY STENTON

ISBN 978-1-61599-453-3   paperback
ISBN 978-1-61599-454-0   hardcover
ISBN 978-1-61599-455-7   eBook

Published by Modern History Press
5145 Pontiac Trail
Ann Arbor, MI 48105

www.ModernHistoryPress.com
info@ModernHistoryPress.com
Tollfree (CAN/USA/PR): 888-761-6268
FAX 734-663-6861

Distributed by Ingram (USA/CAN/AUS), Bertram's Books (UK/EU)

Library of Congress Cataloging-in-Publication Data

Names: Carson, Rugged Dude, 1963- author. | Stenton, Murray, illustrator.
Title: Are you rugged or unrugged? / by Rugged Dude Carson ; illustrated by
    Murray Stenton.
Description: Ann Arbor : Modern History Press, 2019. | Summary: "The
    author's dialectic attempts address the core of what defines ruggedness
    in the male psyche by a series of questions and answers of humorous
    intent. Each hand-drawn panel presents a different scenario where the
    question "Are you rugged or unrugged?" can be asked"-- Provided by
    publisher.
Identifiers: LCCN 2019012358 (print) | LCCN 2019980122 (ebook) | ISBN
    9781615994533 (paperback) | ISBN 9781615994540 (hardcover) | ISBN
    9781615994557 (kindle edition)
Subjects: LCSH: Men--Humor. | Masculinity--Humor.
Classification: LCC PN6231.M45 C38 2019 (print) | LCC PN6231.M45 (ebook)
    | DDC 818/.602--dc23
LC record available at https://lccn.loc.gov/2019012358
LC ebook record available at https://lccn.loc.gov/2019980122

SPECIAL THANKS TO

Mark Baker
The Cutler Family
The Jazic Family
The Telfer Family

If you carry hand sanitizer on your hunting trip so you don't "pick something up," you are unrugged!

If you go through the Tim Horton's drive-thru with a dead deer on the back of your four-wheeler, you are rugged!

If you keep a Harlequin romance novel in your backpack, "just in case" the hunting is slow, you are unrugged!

If your chainsaw is more important to you than your first cousin, you are rugged!

UNRUGGED

If you decide to get a cat rather than a Golden retriever, you are unrugged!

If you remove your artificial leg and use it to kill an attacking wolf, you are rugged!

UNRUGGED

Massage Room

Complimentary Shampoo and conditioner.

If you like going to a KOA campground because they have showers and flush toilets, you are unrugged!

If you convert your snowblower into a ride-on with an empty case of beer and an old pallet, you are rugged!

If you traded in your 4WD truck for a Smart Car because you were fed up with the price of gas, you are unrugged!

If you've ever used duct tape to patch a canoe, you are rugged!

If you iron your hunting pants before wearing them, you are unrugged!

If you catch 10 walleyes with the same minnow, you are rugged
(and so is your minnow)!

If you decide against going fishing because it's "a little too chilly out there," you are unrugged!

If your idea of applying make-up is putting camo make-up on your face before goose hunting, you are rugged!

If you go to the opera with your "Prius driving" neighbours, you are unrugged!

If your idea of a honeymoon is going moose hunting in the Yukon,
you are rugged!

If you think adding camo duct tape to your baby blue scooter makes it cool, you are unrugged!

If you are late getting to school every single morning of duck hunting season, you are rugged!

UNRUGGED

If you would rather stay home and watch reruns of Saved by the Bell instead of going out for the opening day of dove season, you are unrugged!

If you shot a squirrel in the head with a sling shot at 100 feet because you were "pretty sure" you could and wanted to find out for sure, you are rugged!

UNRUGGED

If you're eating around the campfire and actually ask if there are any napkins, you are unrugged!

If you spend more time each week hunting than you do household chores and helping your kids with their homework - combined - you are rugged!

If you think that gutting a deer would be "yucky," you are unrugged!

RUGGED

If you've ever used fishing line and a straightened hook to stitch a wicked cut on your arm, you are rugged!

If you even own one Hawaiian shirt, you are urugged!

If you pull out your skinning knife to cut your steak at the local Outback Steakhouse, you are rugged!

If you are afraid to try fishing because you're worried that your hook might hurt the fish's mouth, you are unrugged!

If you don't even know what a vegan is, you are rugged!

If you need to use half a gallon of gasoline to get a decent campfire going, you are unrugged!

RUGGED

If fly fishing just isn't a challenge to you anymore and you would rather go spear fishing, you are rugged!

If you use Fleecy when you wash your hunting clothes so they "smell fresh," you are unrugged!

If you use an axe to open a can of beans, you are rugged!

RUGGED DUDE CARSON

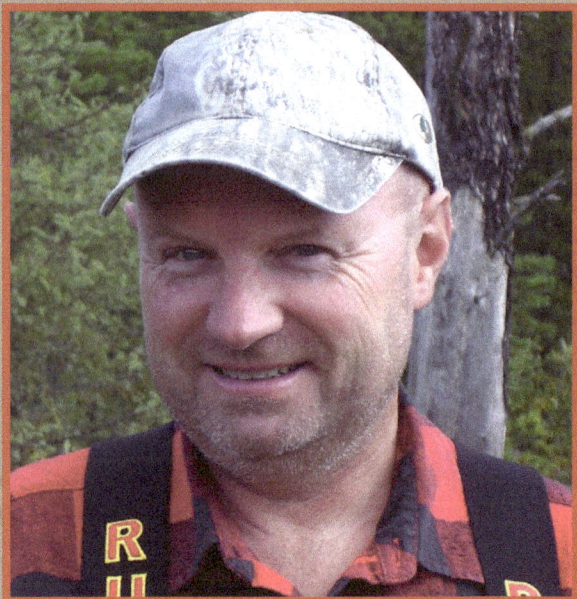

RD, the "Rugged Dude," originally from Ottawa, Ontario, is a Canadian television personality and award winning writer. Starting in 2001, while living in northwestern Ontario, he spent ten years in the media industry hosting and writing a comedy-based fishing and hunting series called "Officially Rugged with RD." The program was broadcast to 60 million households in seven countries for eight seasons. In 2006, RD hosted a radio feature and published a magazine. In 2010, he appeared on the Food Network cooking along-side Bobby Flay, and in 2016, he appeared on The Jim Lahey and Randy Show (of the Trailer Park Boys) on their Swearnet Channel.

In 2007, RD wrote a hunting and fishing guide training program, which he taught in various locations across Canada. He has also spent many days guiding both hunters and fishermen from around the world.

In 2014, RD left northwestern Ontario and moved to Nova Scotia, where he currently lives off-grid, two miles from the nearest road. He spends his time hunting, fishing and raising and growing his own food. He is also a skilled cook specializing in wild game and fish. And, if you ask him, he'll tell you that he is "rugged!" RD's legal name is Rugged Dude Carson.

MURRAY STENTON

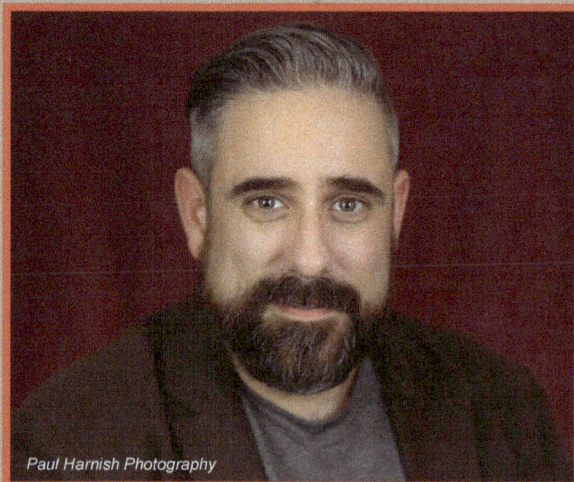

Murray Stenton is a graphic designer and illustrator from Nova Scotia, Canada. For years he has worked as a graphic designer and dabbled in illustration as a hobby. Illustration has been Murray's favorite pastime from an early age. In 2012, Murray had the good fortune of securing his first book illustration contract for a well-known Toronto based children's book author, Jewel Kats. Jewel gave him the opportunity to transform his pastime into a part-time career. With the added confidence of a published work, Murray pursued many more illustration contracts.

This is the first book of this style Murray has had the opportunity to be part of. For Murray, cartooning and creating fun new characters is the most enjoyable part of illustration. Rugged Dude Carson and Murray work well together and hope to continue to work on similar projects in the future.

Paul Harnish Photography

www.ingramcontent.com/pod-product-compliance
Lightning Source LLC
Chambersburg PA
CBHW061412090426

42741CB00023B/3494